Praise for *The Activi*

"Here is another provocative and transformative book by William Martin. This simple yet brilliant interpretation and application of the ancient classic the Tao Te Ching suggests a more sensitive and sensible approach to struggles we all face in today's mercurial, uncertain world. I intend to use his wisdom to make a difference in my professional environment of athletics, addressing the universal issues of money, power, and greed."

— Jerry Lynch, PhD, author of
Coaching with Heart and *Let Them Play*

The
ACTIVIST'S
Tao Te Ching

The

ACTIVIST'S

Tao Te Ching

Ancient Advice for a
MODERN REVOLUTION

WILLIAM MARTIN

New World Library
Novato, California

New World Library
14 Pamaron Way
Novato, California 94949

Text design by Tona Pearce-Myers

Library of Congress Cataloging-in-Publication Data
Names: Martin, William, 1944– author.
Title: The activist's Tao Te Ching : ancient advice for a modern revolution /
    William Martin.
Description: Novato, CA : New World Library, 2016.
Identifiers: LCCN 2016006218 | ISBN 9781608683925 (alk. paper)
Subjects: LCSH: Laozi. Dao de jing. | Philosophy, Chinese—To 221 B.C.
Classification: LCC BL1900.L35 M3645 2016 | DDC 299.5/1482—dc23
LC record available at http://lccn.loc.gov/2016006218

First printing, May 2016
ISBN 978-1-60868-392-5
Ebook ISBN 978-1-60868-393-2
Printed in Canada on 100% postconsumer-waste recycled paper

New World Library is proud to be a Gold Certified Environmentally
Responsible Publisher. Publisher certification awarded by Green Press
Initiative. www.greenpressinitiative.org

10   9   8   7   6   5   4   3   2   1

To Lao-Tzu — ancient myth, legend, teacher, poet,
rabble-rouser, anarchist, and sage:
You have been my guide, brother, father, and uncle,
with never a word of condemnation
or expectation that I should be
other than what I am.
I have written of you and talked about you all my life,
but never really thanked you.

Thank you.

[CONTENTS]

[INTRODUCTION]

Lao-Tzu's classic book of wisdom, the Tao Te Ching, has been my companion for over four decades. I have written interpretations of it for specific modern audiences, such as parents, couples, sages, and caregivers. I hope these interpretations have been of help to people. Writing them has certainly been a helpful and growth-filled experience for me.

Now, as I enter my seventieth year, I feel a new, somewhat unexpected energy emerging from the pages of the Tao Te Ching. Once again, the words of Lao-Tzu, written over 2,500 years ago, are overturning my comfortable assumptions and calling me to a deeper and more active role than I would have dreamed possible. I have always valued the quietism that is inherent in the Tao Te Ching. It is crucial that modern human beings learn to resist the desire to control things by force and violence. Yet my appreciation for the quietist element of Lao-Tzu's writing can lead me to neglect the activism that is also inherent within the Way of Tao. There are occasions when the Tao flows with the crashing, cleansing force of a rushing river, sweeping away all forms in its path. Our world is experiencing one of those occasions. The movement of Tao is gathering its Yang, or active power, for a transformation that will change the world.

As I write these words, the calendar year is reaching a tipping point. It is mid-June, and soon the moment will come when the sun will begin to rise a minute or so later each day and set a minute or so earlier. The difference at first will hardly be noticeable, but before long it will be apparent that the wheel of Yin and Yang is turning toward the darkness of Yin.

Such tipping points are essential to the movement of the Tao. Everything is in a dynamic balance and is constantly adjusting itself in an infinite, intricate dance in which every movement leads to a countermovement. The tipping point is that moment when the ebb and flow are poised for the return movement: ebb begins to flow, flow begins to ebb.

We are living in a time of multiple tipping points. The climate of our planet has already reached a tipping point and has begun the process of restoring a new dynamic of balance. Whether or not this new balance will provide a place for the human race remains to be seen. The gap between the very wealthy and the rest of the world's population has widened and is nearing a tipping point where dissatisfaction and unrest will begin to create the need for change. The energy of a consumer society is nearing the tipping point where the accumulation of trinkets and toys will be exhausted, as will the spirits of those caught in the treadmill of earning more to buy more.

I have reached a personal tipping point in the past year as well. There is a turning in my own understanding of the Tao and in the expressions of it that are emerging in my life. I have begun to paint in the Sumi-e tradition — a meditative use of ink and brush in monochrome tones. It is an art that somehow seems important in a culture of brash colors and sounds that assail the senses at every turn. It slows me down and reminds me of the intrinsic value of art and craft. My writing, both prose and poetry, is taking on a different tone. In many ways, Lao-Tzu's Taoism is quiet and unobtrusive, but each chapter of the Tao Te Ching contains a revolutionary edge that, if lived out, would transform all aspects of society. The flow of Tao in me is tipping from a withdrawn reclusiveness to an activist energy that is fueled by a sense of "things have to change!"

Society has been too long out of balance. Whether or not the human race will notice, and we will align ourselves with this return to balance, is not clear. If we are able to do so, we will find ourselves experiencing a new sense of freedom and justice in all parts of the globe. If we are not able to do so, we will be swept aside and the Tao will restore balance to the planet without us. There has never been a more important time in human history.

Transformation and revolution accompanied the teachings of Taoism in Lao-Tzu's time as well. He wrote and taught sometime just before, or right at the start of, the "Warring States" period of China's history, when the imperial consolidation of power in the hands of a few powerful states and leaders was occurring. It was a time when sacrifice for the state was considered a primary duty.

Lao-Tzu's philosophy of life stood in stark contrast to the structural Confucianism that permeated his society. The rural traditions of China were giving way to urbanization — to the amassing of power and wealth in the hands of a few and the exploitation of the peasant farmers to provide for the cities at the expense of their own communities and families. Even 2,500 years ago, the accumulation of wealth was the priority, and the movement of goods over vast distances was essential to this accumulation. Jobs replaced natural work and the flow of resources began to siphon to the top rather than circulating within the local community. Confucian philosophy supported this consolidation of power in urban areas, while Taoist followers remained distrustful of any authority outside of that which emerged naturally from rural and forest environments. Lao-Tzu's voice was the voice of the peasant, the farmer, and the craftsman — of the vast majority of folk whose desire was for a life of love, simplicity, and contentment. For the past 2,500 years, his work has been revered by the common person and dismissed as seditious by the ruling class of China and other nations.

Lao-Tzu had little use for politics, acquisition, or aggression. He felt that the Tao flowed naturally and that the correct human response was to align oneself with that Flow and move with ease and softness through life. He was also a revolutionary. He was clear that, if people moved into alignment with the Tao, they would find themselves living counter to almost every socially accepted norm. They would feel like strangers in a strange land and would need courage and conviction to keep their social conditioning from reasserting its stranglehold on their lives.

His teachings were seen as a threat to the ordered and compliant social structures of Confucian society, and those who followed his way were branded as lazy, antisocial, unpatriotic anarchists because they followed a way of effortless flow, simplicity, and flexibility. They had a tendency to opt out of the societal structures in favor of a more rural, simple, and cooperative way of life. They sometimes opposed the authority structure, but often they chose to simply ignore it, feeling that the Tao did not seek notice but went about its purpose hidden and without fanfare.

Lao-Tzu felt that leadership must be unnoticed and hidden and must not seek power. He saw the danger of charismatic leaders who could accomplish great things, gather followings of people, and seem to transform society. But when they would die, the relentless tidal power of social greed, fear, and acquisition would move back in. These leaders would become revered, and once they were honored with statues and memorials, their power would be gone — replaced by a facade, their memory co-opted by the ruling oligarchy.

Rather than urging people to take their place as cogs in the massive social hierarchy, he felt the common person could be trusted to order his or her own life in small local communities in a manner that enabled contentment and happiness. He knew that human beings have a "Te" or "natural virtue" that flows within them; if they can learn to trust it, it will guide their actions along healing and compassionate paths.

Instead of acquiescing to the growing materialism and consolidated economic power of his society, Lao-Tzu spoke against greed, materialism, and acquisitiveness. He saw such qualities as leading inevitably to injustice and inequality. Simplicity, he believed, was necessary to keep a healthy balance in life. Instead of an aggressive effort to accomplish lofty goals, he recommended the way of *wu-wei* — of working without the stressful effort that is always accompanied by resistance and fatigue.

He did not use inspiring speeches and lofty teachings. He saw words too often used as propaganda and argument, distracting people from the truth that can be discovered only in silence and mindful attention. This is why he wrote, in total, only five thousand words — one small book of poetry — in his lifetime, yet that small work has become one of the most translated and published books in history.

So, as I explore the Tao Te Ching in my life today, I find myself alternately filled with passion for change and activism and then soothed by the quiet, silent, flowing, and unstoppable nature of the Tao. I find myself living the paradox of a "Quietist Revolution" as the only possible path for true transformation; it's a path that nurtures both sides of my true nature — the stillness at the center of all things, and the active Yang of mindful, powerful, and effective action.

The transformation that the Tao will bring will not be simply the reformation of systems. It will be the de-systemization of society, allowing for a deeper creativity to flow into human persons and communities. We will not be called to create a new set of "rules" but instead to create a flexible approach to each issue; this approach allows us to tack, back off, start again, revamp, rethink, and find the "way" that is appropriate for each time, place, and circumstance. We do not have to "establish" it for the next issue we might face, but merely continue to trust our intelligence, insight, creativity, and ability to order our lives as they are lived. Of course, we learn from experience, but it is not necessary to solidify old solutions in order to learn from them. Quite the opposite. It is our ability to discover ever-new solutions that is the key to a creative life, not the veneration of past solutions.

I offer this new interpretation of the Tao Te Ching as my contribution to this creative task. It is not a translation but an expression in my own words of my sense of the essence of each original chapter. In each chapter here, the first section is a poetic rendition of the same theme contained in the original Tao Te Ching. The second section is a brief commentary that seeks to open up the theme to our lives in the present day. There will be difficult and dangerous times ahead. Established power structures do not give up their perks and privileges easily. We will need courage and a willingness to sacrifice. We will need a tempered enthusiasm that does not burn us out. We will need organization and community support. But above all else we will need a foundation built on something deeper and stronger than our anger and desire for change, important though these energies may be. We will need to fully experience the paradox of an activism built on quietism. We will need an undergirding confidence in the very nature of Life itself, flowing in and through us. The energy of justice and freedom is inherent in the fabric of our being and is beginning to move in ways we have never imagined. It's the flow of the Tao, and it's going to be the ride of the millennium. I don't want to miss it!

William Martin
Chico, California
June 2015

The
ACTIVIST'S
Tao Te Ching

SPONTANEOUS ACTION

Ideas, concepts, and words
have separated us from life.
Masquerading as friends,
they have made us enemies
of each other.

Free of our own prejudices,
we act with spontaneity.
We move naturally.
We accomplish what is necessary.

Caught in our prejudices,
we act as puppets,
moving in lockstep
to the beat of commerce.

All emerges from the Tao,
all returns to the Tao in time.
Meanwhile darkness deepens,
bringing fear and despair.
Darkness faced, however,
opens into daylight.

There is a transformative movement within the Tao that cannot be stopped, any more than water can be stopped from returning to its ocean home. Dams can be built, but it will seep under, flow over, burst through, or evaporate and rain on the other side. This is the energy we have flowing within and through us.

A QUIET REVOLUTION

Change does not come
from eloquence or persuasion.
When injustice is the rule,
justice always lies in wait.
Where oppression flourishes,
freedom ever lurks.
Where death is the threat,
life springs into being.
The darkness of power,
unknowing, contains the seeds
of a bright new light.

Therefore the people act
but do not force;
they teach without agenda
and let freedom emerge
without conscious effort.

We want justice now! But if we let the Tao flow through
us, it alone will break the dam, sweep away the debris of
greed, and cleanse our culture's wounds. Our role will be to
ride the wave and gently help people find the freedom that
it brings.

WE ARE NOT FOOLED

When a nation values wealth and status,
its citizens are easily controlled
by their desires and their fears.

When we learn to value simple things
and are not enticed by power,
we can open the hearts of people
to the joy of ordinary life.
We will not be fooled by clever words
designed to keep us captive,
promising us a better day,
someday.
When we no longer believe
these empty promises,
already better days
are on their way.

We are not seeking justice just so everyone can share the
trinkets of a consumer culture. We are seeking the freedom
to live without artificially induced desires. When this happens, justice will be natural and flow like a river.

[4]

WITHOUT AGENDA

The Tao is empty of agenda,
therefore full of possibilities.
It is not a limited reservoir of energy,
doled out in parcels to supplicants.
It is an infinite field.
We don't know what the future looks like.
Transformation will surprise us with its form.
If we knew what it would look like,
our vision would be limited
and our efforts would be futile.

We act in service to the formless Tao,
not to the forms and functions of our restless minds.
So we let the tension recede,
our bodies relax,
and our minds open
to the future.

Whatever is impelling us is rooted in a mystery. Whatever is happening to us is not the usual dance. Something new is being shaped that began before time itself was formed. We're not causing it to happen. We're letting it happen in us.

NO PREFERENCES

The Tao has no preferences
and will not "take our side."
Oppressors and oppressed alike
are born within
and carried by the Tao.
New forms are always appearing,
for the Tao is always breathing
fresh new life into being
and giving rest to the old.

We will often feel at war with those who cling to prestige
and power, but it is the nature of power itself that we are
fighting. Oppressor and oppressed will both be free when
the desire for power is laid aside and the forms that support
that power are dismantled.

SURE HOPE

The Tao gave birth
to everything seen and unseen,
to that which came before,
and followed after,
the Big Bang of creation.

The seeds of revolution,
sprouting, blooming, blossoming
within us at this moment,
were scattered in that First Explosion,
gathered in the hearts of stars,
germinated in the oceans of life,
and are born in our hearts today.

Don't give in to frustration and despair. We may not live to
see the day when all are free, but that which began before
the beginning of beginning-less time cannot be thwarted. It
is alive within us and will live on when we are gone.

[8]

TRUE POWER

Controlling power bestows its benefits
only to those who bow before it.
This transformation, however,
flows like a river,
benefiting all in its path,
asking nothing,
withholding from no one.

Therefore we choose to live
in simple dwellings, remaining
close to nature,
and to the earth
that feeds us.
We keep our spirits quiet
and our thoughts without turmoil.
We speak our message clearly
and with compassion.
We manage things without controlling.
We work with mindful concentration.
We compete with no one.

There will be the necessary marches, protests, and organizing. But much of our action will be unnoticed by power. Power will wake one day and discover that people have found their own way, no longer bothered by power's illusions.

[9]

NO PRAISE, NO BLAME

If we have something to lose,
we will not succeed.
We will cling to that thing;
an opinion, a possession,
or our reputation.
Clinging,
we will be vulnerable.
Being vulnerable,
we will remain prisoners to power.

The way ahead is to work each day
then lay aside all thought
of praise or blame
or gain or loss,
and sleep in peace.

We will exhaust ourselves trying to please the multitude of voices clamoring for our attention. Assigning praise or blame to everyone we see, we are playing by the rules of our oppressors, who use our fear of loss to keep us quiet, distracted, and arguing among ourselves.

QUALITIES

Here are the qualities
necessary for a true revolution:

a mind and body unified
in focus and flexibility;
a clear and nonjudgmental vision
that sees the ever-present light;
a courageous kindness that acts,
but remains unsung and unknown;
an open life that lets things come
and go, while remaining undisturbed;
a light-hearted acceptance of oneself,
free of pomposity and self-importance.

If we cultivate these qualities,
we will lead without controlling,
act energetically without forcing,
and gain everything while possessing nothing.

The qualities necessary for lasting change are inner qualities. They will manifest, to be sure, in outer acts, but their
origin is within each person. If society valued and practiced
these qualities, a revolution would not be necessary.

[7]

SUCCESS

How can we succeed
against such terrible power?

Because we do not seek to rule
the people, but to follow them.
Because we do not seek to gain power,
but to remain behind the scenes.
Our fears and desires have become
mere phantoms, ephemeral,
figments that no longer distract.
We have let go of ourselves
and are one with the movement of Tao.
We are without worry about success or failure.

This is how we will succeed.

The desire to change the world is not the energy that will
carry the day. That will narrow our focus and divert our
power. Without desires of our own, we can cooperate with
all the ways the world will heal itself.

I DON'T KNOW

When we unite in our common cause,
we present a visible force
and are taken seriously.
But it is the invisible spirit within us,
seen by no one,
that will do the work.

We have beliefs and convictions
running through our thinking minds,
but it is the spacious place
within these minds, the fertile emptiness,
that will change the world.

We will create new models
by which we live together,
but it will be the room and space
we give each other
that will bring us life.

It is all too easy for us as activists to become "full of our-selves." A self-righteous halo often faintly glows in rooms where we gather, leaving no room for doubt, self-awareness, humility, and openness to new ideas. We fill the space with our wonderful intentions and have no place in which to utter the important phrase, "I don't know…"

INFORMATION OR WISDOM?

Media continuously assaults the senses,
then offers us something to buy
to ease the stress.
The voices clamor for our eyes, hands,
ears, hearts, and bodies,
offering trinkets in return
for vital treasures.

Wisdom sees and hears the outer world,
but acts only at the urgings
of the inner world.

A truism asserts that "information is power." Not really.
Unless information is digested by a spacious heart instead
of a conditioned mind, it is actually disempowering. The
conditioned mind molds information into ammunition to
hurl at opponents and justify our actions. The spacious
heart sifts information carefully, not letting it overwhelm
or confuse us, but making sure it carefully guides us along
helpful paths.

HOPE AND FEAR

Both hope and fear are hollow companions.
Each will trigger anxious thoughts.
If hope and fear drive us,
our actions will be built on unstable ground.
We will always second-guess our moves,
looking over our shoulder, fearful
even of our friends,
squabbling among ourselves,
blaming and praising in a futile attempt
to control people and events.

Only when we see ourselves and the world
as "One Thing Happening"
will our fears and hopes subside.
We act upon the world,
but are not separate from it.
We are not healing the world from afar.
We are part of the world,
healing itself.

We don't have to hope for freedom and justice in our world, nor fear for their lack. The Taoist knows that the Tao will unfailingly bring balance to the world, but we do not know the how or the when of that process, nor what the next form will be. We are simply doing, in perfect freedom, that which is ours to do.

FORMLESS FLOW

The change that is coming
did not start in some particular place
nor at a particular time.
It began when the Tao
Big-Banged itself into form,
and it has been carried in the stardust
that now makes up our bodies.

Don't look for beginnings or endings,
but find the seamless, formless Flow
that is returning always to the center
where peace and justice wait.

We don't have to make it happen.
It is happening as I write
and as you read.
When we both look up,
there it will be,
waiting for us
to simply do what's next.

This is the paradox of true activism. We don't force, push, or strain, for these are actions of the separate ego. Still, the power that moves us cannot be stopped. We don't push, but neither do we turn aside and pretend that our actions are not necessary. They are necessary, but they are truly helpful only when they arise from a deeper level than our ego-centric mind.

UNLIKELY REBELS

Those who would truly change the world
do not seem like rebels.
They are deliberate and careful,
aware of every nuance
and movement around them.
They are kind and courteous in conversation.
There is a lovely simplicity about them,
something selfless and disarming,
welcoming and accepting,
and above all, clear.

They are willing to wait patiently
until proper action arises by itself,
then they move with surprising
swiftness and power.
Though their lives are at risk,
they are calm and unworried,
because they are truly free.

This revolution is like none that has come before. This one
will happen with, or without, our help. Thus we are free to
act without needing to push, pull, force, or convince. Our
muscles will be relaxed, our speech will be gentle, and our
actions will be filled with power.

RETURN TO SOURCE

Revolution is not simply a turning over;
it is a returning to the Source.
Having strayed from the Source,
our world falters and flails
about for balance.

Therefore we calm ourselves,
let our thoughts become still,
and watch the way all things
are seeking this return.
At the still point of our lives,
we act decisively, but without judgment;
we confront power, but without hatred;
we see all things distinctly,
yet we know that they are all One Thing.
We are ready to live with joy
and die without regret.

This Source to which we are returning is neither a religious
ideal nor a separate deity. It is simply the nature of life itself,
which has always been just "One Thing Happening." No
doubt we will be involved in concrete actions of compassion
and confrontation, but we will always know, somewhere in
our deepest parts, that we are part of just One Thing.

ALL BY OURSELVES

The most effective leader
is unknown and unsung.
Honor and respect
from followers and crowds
feels exciting and powerful,
but the trap of conditioned ego
waits along this path.
Inspiring fear and hate
also feels like power,
but the trap here
is already sprung.

Because our actions
do not call attention to ourselves,
when it is over, people will say,
"Look at what we did all by ourselves!"
And they will be right.

We all enjoy honor and affirmation. This is not a bad thing.
Do your daily work with compassion and care, and this will
be honor enough. When it comes to a revolution, the more
you seek to be noticed, the less effective you will be. These
leadership principles themselves are revolutionary.

STRUCTURES

Without the Tao,
these things arise:
clever schemes,
rules for behavior,
laws for control,
demands for loyalty,
and the facade of patriotism.
With the Tao,
all goodness and virtue
arises from within the heart.

We are not forcing justice and fairness
upon an unwilling crowd.
We are freeing these natural qualities
waiting within each person.

If we build new structures to insure that people obey our
own ideas of "the way things should be," we will be wasting
our time. Before long we will be facing yet another revolution — this time aimed at us.

DECREASE

The path to freedom and justice
can be summed up in the principle
"decrease in order to increase."
Decrease what you want,
and decrease what you have.
You will then find what you truly desire,
and you will have everything you need.

When people are truly free,
they will naturally move toward simplicity
without needing to be told,
coerced, or manipulated.

The key to a truly revolutionary life is the power of simple
living. We must show that we follow this path by the way we
order our lives. The way of "decrease" is so contrary to the
consumer/capitalist values of our world, might we one day
face suspicion and arrest simply for not shopping enough?

BREAD AND CIRCUSES

As in Roman days,
we are kept in thrall
by bread and circuses.
Fast food and football games
keep our stomachs stuffed
and our minds saturated
with the need to win.
And when amusements fail,
we are made to be afraid.
Together, these three —
bread, circuses, and fear —
keep us under control.

Only when we cease to care
about the things we're told to value
will we find the stillness and the freedom
of a quiet, undisturbed, and peaceful mind.

The tactics of control are subtle and effective. Never underestimate the power of conditioning. Even our desire for

a transformation will be used to stir us up, pointing us first this way, then that way, until we are running around in circles. A monastic quality of stillness is necessary if we are to be free of the sophisticated mind control on which society has been built.

A LIGHT WITHIN

True revolutionaries
must be at one with the Tao.

This work will take us into dark,
hidden, and unknown places;
places where we can't see
the way ahead.
Our ego won't know the way.
The only light we'll know
will be found deep within us.
This light's been there
since the dawn of time.
It can be trusted.

Our mind has much to do as we organize, plan, speak, and act. But it won't carry us through the difficulties and discouragements that lie ahead. The systems we oppose will seek to make us feel isolated, alone, and powerless. Sometimes they will succeed. We will have to trust that an inexpressible and unfathomable power is in the very atoms of our being and will do, through us, that which is necessary.

THE ACCEPTANCE PARADOX

Acceptance of what is
is the only path to change.
We must accept,
with clear and calm awareness,
that our world is gravely wounded,
dysfunctional, and deluded.
We must not turn our eyes away,
pretending not to notice.
We must not believe that if we grit our teeth,
and try a little harder to make things work,
that all will turn out fine.
We must empty ourselves of hope
that the road our world is traveling
will lead to peace and freedom.
We must abandon all the things
that we've been told will lead to satisfaction.
We must give up trying to be right,
and let the Tao begin to live our life.
Only then will space appear,
an empty womb in which
a new world might be born.

The belief that accepting things as they are means that they will never change is a misunderstanding of the power of acceptance. For instance, not until we accept abuse — and let go of the hope that, if we did things a bit better or spoke more gently, we could somehow change the other person — will we be able to clearly see our options. Until we abandon hope, we will not see the path opening ahead of us.

PERSPECTIVE

Keep things in perspective
and live as if the world we want
has already come to be.
Let our words and actions
express the essence of the changes
we may never live to see.
Nothing we create will last.
It will have its place, then disappear.
So let's build it with joy,
establish it with compassion,
and hold it in our open hands.

Clinging to our work will constrict its effectiveness. Clinging to our ideas will limit their scope. Clinging to our forms
and structures will make them into the very institutions we
have vowed to leave behind.

BE COMPLETELY WHO WE ARE

The more we try to change things,
the more they stay the same.
The more we push and prod them,
the firmer they remain.
The more eloquent we try to sound,
the less and less we're heard.

The freedom we are seeking
is contained within our very nature.
There is no way to force things into being.
The only thing we need to do
is be completely who we are,
in every breath, and word, and moment.

We are not trying to "get things done." We must learn to let the changes "do themselves" — to see the path of action unfold before us and move along that path with the unhurried, yet unstoppable, power of the Tao.

THE WOMB OF TAO

The Cosmos, in all its fiery explosive wonder,
delicately balances the Yin and Yang
in which all that is, was, and will ever be
moves and flows in harmony.
The Origin of the Cosmos has no name,
but when we speak of it, we call it "Tao."

To change our human future,
we must give honor to the Earth.
The Earth, in turn, depends upon
the movement of the Cosmos.
The Cosmos rests within the womb of Tao.
So, any changes we seek to make
must have their origins within that womb.

A mystery surrounds our efforts. We have started on a path
of change and transformation. Something new is being born
within our lives that is as fundamental as the dawning of the
Copernican revolution. The very nature of humanity and
society will be affected by the simple work that we've begun. Don't underestimate the power of this day, these times,
and this opportunity.

DISTRACTION

The mind is like a stray dog
in a whistlers' convention.
The poor thing is summoned
by a multitude of commands:
"Here," "Here," "Over here…"

We must be led by an internal compass
that is unaffected by the myriad winds that rise
to blow us here and there.
Restless energy will weaken our efforts.
Distractions will seem important
but will dissipate our energy.

We don't have to leave ourselves
to change the world.
We only have to *be* ourselves.

There is so much that needs doing, changing, healing, and
fixing. Our good intentions keep us on the surface of the
wheel of change, spinning round and round. Yet the only
thing that actually needs doing is the simple task that is
directly in our path, right here, right now.

THE SECRET

No blueprint, yet the future arrives.
No argument, yet people change.
We act according to our intuition
and find the way unfolds before us.
In the darkness around us,
we have an inner light as guide.
We walk the path to unknown places
and are surprised that people follow us.

We have learned the secret of transformation:
Injustice feeds our determination.
Hate increases our love.
Wounds bring forth our healing,
and fear uncovers our courage and serenity.

Part of us would love to plot and scheme in darkened rooms,
speaking in code and trusting no one. Such things will never
bring about the change for which we long. The secret is:
There is no secret. We do what is ours to do, and we help
other people do the same.

EMBRACING EVERYTHING

Letters, speeches, and demonstrations
might be useful tools,
but they must have their roots
within the quiet of our souls.

When activism unites
with the quiet place inside us,
a circuit is completed.
The energy of the Tao begins to flow.
Nothing can oppose it
because it embraces everything.
In our work we must always seek
to unite all that seems divided.

To do our work in the world, we divide things into pieces.
Then we move the pieces around to see if we can build
something new, something that brings benefit and justice
to all people. We arrange and rearrange the pieces, seeking
the most helpful alignment. But always remember that the
pieces are arbitrary divisions, superimposed on a Great
Unity. It is from this Unity that we gain our power.

NO OBJECTIVES

To have concrete objectives
is to treat some things as objects
and to see ourselves as separate.
Since separation is the root of our problem,
our efforts will be futile.

Transformation cannot be controlled.
It will proceed in its own way,
at its own pace.
Fast, slow, success, failure,
strength, weakness —
all take their natural place.

How, then, are we to proceed?
How do we know what to do
and not to do?
We trust the moment.
We work and rest,
succeed and fail,
without undue ado.

Of course, we have intentions, plans, and specific things to do. But we don't assume our plans must succeed or all is lost. There is a lightness and serenity in our work that prevents the classic activist disease of chronically tightened sphincter muscles. Our smile muscles get more exercise than our frown muscles, and our messiah complex disappears.

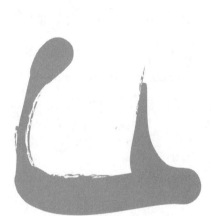

SUBVERSION

Taking arms against oppression
seems sometimes so necessary,
but force will always replace
one oppression with another.
The damage done will be the seed
of more injustice and despair.

Ours is a "Quietist Revolution,"
an oxymoronic truth we cannot avoid.
We work from the bottom,
not the top.
Our actions are focused and hidden,
not forced and trumpeted.
We will overcome without triumphing.

Subversion means "a turning from below." It is one of the most powerful tools of the Taoist revolutionary. The changes in direction and momentum we seek will begin in hidden places, unnoticed, subtly changing the living and consuming patterns of our communities, leaving the oppressive systems robbed of power. It will be like a river that changes its course, leaving behind the dry channel in which it was once confined.

WEAPONS

To hold a weapon feels empowering.
The sleek and deadly steel seduces
with its promise of potency
in the face of tyranny.
It is an empty promise,
one that will destroy our dream.
If we clutch weapons to our breasts,
the tyranny will seep within our souls,
and we will become
the very thing we fear.

There may be times when,
faced by unavoidable violence,
we must respond in kind.
But a victory gained by force of arms
must never lead to parades and celebrations,
but to tears that this has happened.

If our creative and alternative ways of living come to be
perceived as such a threat that violence is brought against
us, it may be necessary to respond. If so, we must remember
that the humans we are fighting are simply fellow victims of
delusion and fear.

ONE THING

No thing exists in and of itself.
Every thing is part of Something Else.
The subtle distinctions that we devise
obscure the truth of what is happening.
The most important change of all
will be the way we see and think.
When people begin to see the Whole,
instead of just the so-called parts,
harmony and peace will come,
not through rules and laws,
but through the natural goodness
of the human heart, freed at last
from false distinctions.

There is a mystical element in our path that causes some to
turn aside with cries of "airy-fairy New Age nonsense." Far
from being "New Age," this element is rooted in an ancient
understanding of the wholeness of the Cosmos, in which
every "thing" emerged from One Thing. Without a trust in
essential wholeness, there can be no lasting transformation.

[33]

WITHIN OURSELVES

Intelligent people know the problems of the world
and point to those who seem to cause the problems.
Wise people know the origins of the problems
within the workings of the mind.
Forceful people overcome their opposition.
People with true power
overcome the lies told within the mind
and bring about the only true,
enduring freedom.

Intelligence is a true asset and should not be overlooked.
Yet the chaotic social reality of the planet is overseen by intelligent people who have abandoned wisdom. Every bit of
chaos and injustice has its origins in the fear and sense of
separation that is born within the mind. We must see and
heal it in ourselves before we can heal it in others.

[34]

HIDDEN POWER

Ours will be a humble revolution.
No powerful leaders generating veneration,
subtly stealing our own power from us.
No great campaigns or slogans.
No billions raised for media buys.

Like the Tao, our power hides itself
so it can work unnoticed down within
the hearts and minds of common people.
Hidden, yet filling everything.
Powerful, yet not controlling.

What could stop such power?

The decisive battles will not be covered by television. No
movement or person will siphon off the natural power that
is arising even now within the collective mind of humankind. When that power begins to flow, it will move like
water into every nook and cranny of society, transforming
everything, owning nothing.

ENGROSSED BUT EXHAUSTED

Wars distract our anger and fear,
pointing us to an enemy of convenience.
Media bypasses our intelligence,
feeding illusion directly to our brains.
Conditioned to trade our precious time
for a little bit of money,
we trudge along in service to a dream
that is not ours.
We are kept engrossed and distracted
but too exhausted to see
the cliff edge drawing near.

We are told: "It's too complicated for you to understand.
Trust us, we have all the facts and will take care of things.
Just keep your focus on your job. Work hard and be loyal to
us, and we promise that we will take care of you." Change
will come when we stop believing it!

NEW FOUNDATIONS

A society that rises too high
will fall;
that extends too far
will contract;
that gathers too much
will lose it all.
This is the natural way of things.

Force will not be necessary.
The renewal we seek is part
of the natural way of life.

Our work will be hidden and subtle
but it will bring healing to all.

The sickness and weakness of our society has become clear
to us. The pomp, opulence, and arrogance we see displayed
are undermined by injustice, poverty, and discontent. The
foundations are crumbling. Brash polemics can no longer
sustain the system. Our task is not to destroy society, for it
is dying on its own. We must offer healing and the tools to
build a world on new foundations.

[37]

SILENCE

Noise confounds our leaders.
They don't know what to do.
Scurrying this way, then that,
they never find the silent Tao
within.
If they could find that silence,
the country would transform itself.
Simplicity and freedom from desire
would become the natural way,
and destructive habits would fall away,
replaced by patient compassion for all of life.

Leaders will never find that silence while serving the current system. Since dollars have become speech, the noise has overwhelmed all possibility of silence. No one in leadership has ears to hear the quiet amid the cacophony of special interests. New systems must be founded on a stillness, a serenity where decisions can be considered from a place of wisdom, not from urgency or expediency. Of course, we can't form such systems until we find a silent place within ourselves.

NO RULES

Feeling separate from their true nature,
people urge each other to be good and moral.
Failing at that, people demand
that everyone act with justice.
Failing at justice, we insist
that everyone obey the rules.
Failing that, we settle for pretending
that nice-sounding words will do.

Goodness, morality, and justice
will flow someday from the fountain
deep within the individual heart.
They won't be forced by rules,
bound by laws, or separated from community.

Aren't some rules and expectations necessary for societal life? Of course. But they must emerge from the meeting of individual hearts within a community, serve a specific need for the expression of compassion, and be modified or dropped when they no longer meet or express that purpose.

LEADERS

Was there ever a time
when leaders were humble,
seeking to be of service,
and taking the lowest places
at the table?
Was there a time
when they eschewed reward,
needed no adulation,
and refused gifts?
Was there ever a time
when leaders were simply common stones,
rolling along with the rest of us
in the river?

The leaders we desire are those whose lives are rooted in the Tao, by whatever name they call it. If they were to be found, all the world would live in natural peace, contentment, and joy. They would consider themselves little children, despite their seeming power, dependent on the Tao and helpless without it. When leaders lose their humanity, how can the world become humane?

NO US

All our plans and dreams
will someday return,
along with us,
to the Tao.
The Tao is the origin of all things,
and the destiny of all things.
This is why we do our work
with confidence and peace.

There is no "us." There is no "them" against whom we
fight. We are simply part of the movement of Tao. We plan,
hope, dream, and work as if our contentment were at stake.
But, in fact, we are already content to be who, and what, and
where we are — doing what we're doing because... well,
simply because it's what is ours to do.

[41]

PARADOX ABOUNDS

Some people, a few, think things are fine
just as they are, and laugh at change.
Most people know that change is necessary
but spend their time looking for other people
to blame or someone to fix the problem for them.

Some people know that change is necessary,
and they begin to live that change
within themselves.

So paradox abounds in transformation:
True clarity will seem confusing to most.
True advancement will seem like going backward.
True power will be flexible and receptive.
True strength will appear as weakness.
True goodness will be suspect.
True wisdom will be open to learning.

I have a Che Guevara T-shirt. I wear it just to remind
myself that revolutionaries are complex, misunderstood,
heroic, brutal, idolized, and vilified. Our revolution will not
look like Che's. In the Tao, appearances will be deceiving.
Some will cheer. Many will stand by and shake their heads.
Some will laugh. A few will roll up their sleeves and get to
work.

BALANCE

Transformation is not the same as progress.
Evolution is a winding path
that sometimes goes in one direction,
then reverses course.
We will sometimes make great strides,
and feel that a new world is near at hand,
only to find our expectations dashed
and have to start again from scratch.

This is the Way of Tao,
and nothing can exist without this dance
of Yin and Yang together.
When loss and deprivation come,
we stay at the center of things
and use events for benefit.
When gain and success come,
we stay at the center of things
and use these, too, for benefit.

It is our ability to use events, rather than be swayed to and
fro by them, that will bring success. Forcing events is the

way of oppressors, and this is ultimately a futile way of living. Whenever events are forced too far in one direction, they will snap back with surprising force and power. We must find the balance point in the flow of things, much like a surfer who lets the power of the wave do all the work and merely guides the board with the subtlest of movements.

STILLNESS

Stillness brings results
that action cannot achieve.
Quietness can accomplish more
than angry words.
In a noisy, restless, raging world,
such qualities are rare,
yet they are the only path
to lasting transformation.

Stillness is a difficult practice. We want change *now*, and we will inundate people with our protest marches and our polemics until we get what we want. This is understandable. We have watched our world sink into chaos and injustice for too long. There will, of course, be times of forceful action, but the power of a "Quietist Revolution" will come from the depth of our stillness and the serenity of our quiet hearts.

SIREN SONGS

Wealth, fame, and power
are the siren songs of culture,
echoing throughout the day
in countless subtle ways.
They have lured our world onto the rocks
of greed, oppression, and chaos,
and they remain the most dangerous obstacles
to the work of transformation.

Only contentment with the simple things in life
will insulate us from their allure.
Only generosity of spirit
will allow us to withstand their power.

These temptations are powerful because they are hidden
within high-minded phrases. If we see ourselves as virtu-
ous, exemplary, and noble, we may succeed in remaking
society, but it will end up just the same inside.

THE COMMON MAN

People strive to take the direct
and shortest route
to what they want.
The road that we are taking
will seem to twist and wind,
but it is the only way to justice.
People seek to appear exceptional,
a cut above the common man.
Our way appears quite ordinary,
but it requires great skill.
People love to hear confident words
spoken without doubt or hesitation.
Our words, however, are tentative
yet are exactly what is needed.

So many activists talk about "the common man," but most see themselves as exceptional and gifted: leaders, not followers. Those who speak and act with total confidence are prey to arrogance. People speak of them with admiration, but they are secretly waiting for them to trip and fall. And they always do.

[46]

CONTENTMENT

Contentment is not our goal.
Contentment is our starting point.
Content to be alive.
Content to be who we are,
at this time, in this place.
Content to be doing this work.

Contentment leads to the creation
of helpful tools and actions.
Discontentment leads to making
weapons, walls, and war.

It is not dissatisfaction that drives us. Of course, we are dissatisfied with what we see happening in our chaotic world, and we work to create just and humane structures and processes. But this dissatisfaction is not what gives us power. Our acceptance of our particular time, place, self, and work is what makes us powerful. We are not looking for "something else" to make us happy. We are happy to give our lives to walk this path.

THE WORLD INSIDE

The whole world of oppression,
injustice, hunger, sickness,
greed, hate, and war can be seen
without turning on the TV,
without reading the news,
without browsing the internet,
and without even going outside.
Attend carefully to every flicker of thought
that flashes in your mind.
Begin your revolutionary work here.

Nothing "out there" is alien to the mind. The seeds of compassion coexist with the seeds of cruelty. Our world has watered and nurtured the latter and ignored the former. The place we begin to reverse that process is within our own minds.

[48]

LAID ASIDE

Those who join a revolution
with the secret hope of gaining
something for themselves
are merely conducting a business enterprise.
Only when all hope of gain is set aside
can one be truly revolutionary.

Instead of seeking gain,
each day we let something drop away.
We carry less and less that way,
and one day we will wake to find
there is nothing more to carry.

Our expectations of what we want a new, transformed, and equitable world to be like will only slow us down. Worrying about our place in this new world will only diminish our power. In a truly transformed life, possessions, thoughts, anxieties, goals, and anything else that impedes the expression of authentic, unforced, effortless action is gradually laid aside.

IDEALS

We are not contending with enemies.
We hold no rigid agendas,
so people are able to see their own way.
We trust the people,
even when they disappoint us.
We tell the truth,
even when we are lied to.
We are compassionate,
even when we are hated.
This is why our work will succeed.

The revered ideals of humankind — compassion, truth, trust, and cooperation — are spoken of by many but lived by very few. When the crunch comes, our conditioned response is to self-protect and use whatever force, deceit, and manipulation are necessary to achieve our aims. This is why the history of revolution has been without lasting success. Intentions are good, even noble. But circumstances force compromises. Fear forces defenses to be built. Lack of trust forces deceit. Let's be careful out there.

LIFE AND DEATH

The artificial separation of life and death
creates a society of distraction,
obsession, and avoidance
and leaves people prey to exploitation.
"Look over here!" the voices clamor.
"Be very afraid!" they whisper.
"Better not to think about it," they declare.
"Trust us. We will keep you safe," they insinuate.

When life and death have become the same,
a revolution will occur.

I use the word *revolution* knowing that it carries many images. However, a radical transformation of the fossilized
structures of society is an unavoidable reality, no matter
what we call it. Ceasing to believe the deeply ingrained
messages that seem so real, so true, is a "turning over" of
monumental proportions. Unless we let go of everything
we thought we knew about living and dying, nothing will
change. We will remain captive.

NOT ALONE

You are an expression of the Tao,
arising at this particular time,
in this particular form,
in this particular place,
to add your contribution
to this revolution.

There is an energy flowing in you
that cultivates, nurtures,
and prepares you for your work;
comforts and fortifies you in your efforts;
and guides you to completion.

We are none of us alone. We are not billiard balls careening around a table, bouncing off one another, trying to get one another to go along the path we think is right. We are the Tao, guiding the world along a path of restoration; at the same time we are guided by a mysterious inner light that illumines all of life. Compose your mind and unknot your muscles. Enjoy the unique work you have to do.

SHUT THE GATES

We cannot transform the world
without knowing our own true nature.
We must see beyond the noise and confusion
and become aware of the silent womb
in which all things are formed.

This is our home, our Source, and our refuge.
If we can still the yammering voices
that tell us we are small and powerless,
we will find an authority within our hearts,
a capacity within our bodies,
and a light behind our eyes,
that will guide us,
and our world,
safely home.

Lao-Tzu uses the phrase "shut the gates" in several chapters. It is a symbolic way of urging us to turn our attention inward instead of constantly engaging the outer world with our thoughts, opinions, and pronouncements. If we are always conducting a shouting match with our opponents, no one will be able to hear their own authentic voice. In the quiet, we find our origin and our home. We cease being isolated orphans and find ourselves a part of it *all*.

MIND TRAINING

When the rich gather possessions,
and distract themselves with amusements,
taking that which is not given,
while the basic needs of people go unmet,
the world has forgotten the Way of Tao.

This Way is broad, clear, and dependable,
but our mind is trained to lead us round in circles,
going nowhere, accomplishing nothing.

The mind is the source of oppression, but it is also the instrument by which we will free ourselves. The mind naturally wants to follow the Tao, to respond in unforced, natural, and effective ways to the needs of the community. But it has been conditioned by learned fears, upon which those in power depend to keep us docile and compliant. We must notice the subtle ways our thoughts are led down precarious pathways. Only then can we see the path ahead.

WELLSPRING

When the steadfast path of the Tao
is present in our thoughts,
we will not be unnerved
by cataclysmic events.
Upheaval and turmoil are inevitable,
and revolution is inescapable.
But the Tao is everywhere,
and when it is embodied in our person,
our community blossoms and thrives;
when our communities thrive,
nations become havens;
when nations become havens,
our work is done.

It starts with us. From there our work swells in ever-
expanding and unceasing circles. Our work must always
concentrate on our own minds and hearts, and then on our
immediate communities. From there, the circle flows outward with a momentum of its own. Very few of us will ride
the crest of that flow. Most of us will do our work at home,
supplying the wellspring of the power.

THE NATURE OF THINGS

Whatever is forced into existence
will soon fade away.
What is allowed to arise
of its own inherent nature
will remain and prosper.

Therefore, when our work arises
from our own true nature,
we are flexible, yet indestructible;
adaptable, yet powerful;
able to work all day, yet not grow fatigued.

When oppressive forms and systems are imposed, great
force is needed to keep them in place. The effort to keep
them in place is consuming our happiness and our very
planet. When these forms begin to collapse, we will be
ready with alternatives that have grown in natural, effortless ways, nurtured by authentic human spirits; these will
endure.

THOSE WHO TALK DON'T KNOW

The less confidence we feel,
the more we will shout and clamor.
Propaganda is contrary to this path.
We have no need to convince others
by using clever words
and appealing to their emotions.
Our message does not need to hide
behind images of fears foreseen
or of desires unfulfilled.

Conventional wisdom would say we need to grab the spotlight, appeal to the hearts and minds of people, show them the righteousness of our cause, and confront the propaganda of our oppressors with counterpropaganda of our own. But minds that are awakened, even just a bit, to the Oneness of all within the Tao are not fooled by propaganda from either side. These people will see for themselves.

ANARCHY

Here are some closely guarded secrets:
Without rules, people become honest.
Without economics, people become wealthy.
Without religion, people see the world as sacred.
Without trying to change, we ignite a revolution.
Let go of rules.
Let go of economics.
Let go of religion.
Let go of trying to change.

There is a natural anarchy that arises from a trust in the goodness inherent in the nature of people. Lao-Tzu believed in order, but he knew that order must arise from the nature of things rather than from the agendas and programs of those whose primary desire is predictability, order, and control. There will be frightening elements in the coming transformation, but don't be afraid. We will naturally know how to do the things that are good.

A CERTAIN COURAGE

The Tao will bring new order,
but not control;
it will eradicate injustice,
but do no harm.
Likewise, we will have firm principles,
but not harm others in their name.
We will guide people,
but never outshine them.
We will let power emerge from people,
but without interference or control.

The path of a quiet revolutionary may require the courage
to face a violent death, but far more often this courage will
enable us to sit quietly, watch things emerge, and not give in
to restlessness and earnest meddling.

CONNECTED

The new world will be governed with moderation.
Energy will not be wasted on rigid plans and projects.
Power will not be wasted on blame and punishment.
No matter how complicated affairs might seem,
they will be cared for with the gentleness
of a mother caring for a child.
No matter how chaotic things may seem,
we will not get blown about by the winds of confusion
because we are rooted and connected
to the Tao and to one another.

Stand with your feet slightly apart. Relax your shoulders. Let your knees unlock. Let your neck loosen and the muscles of your face soften. Imagine the energy of your body flowing down through your feet into the earth and back again, refreshed and nurtured by your roots. Now imagine all the people in your community doing the same, and imagine the energy intertwining together into "Just One Thing Happening."

[60]

NO FORCE NECESSARY

Approach this most important enterprise
with the patience and care you bring
to the careful preparation of food.
Too much hurry,
too much force,
and the meal is ruined.

Injustice will not disappear overnight,
but each small step will increase
wisdom and judgment.
That, in turn, will bring integrity
and lasting compassion.

It will be hard to let even the smallest injustice go unrecti-
fied, but impatience and overeagerness will meet oppression
with oppression. No one will learn the wisdom necessary
for a lasting transformation. We're not yet wise enough
to create a new society. We will gain the wisdom as we go,
therefore we must not let restlessness push us into actions
that we will later rue.

NO ARGUMENT

Stillness and lowliness will prevail,
while noise and grandeur will fail.
There will be no need to recruit others,
nor convince them to join our cause.
No need to argue or force;
simply walk along our path less taken
and extend support to those
who choose to walk as well.

Very few people are persuaded by argument. Argument is generally two fixed opinions battering each other with facts and emotions, neither truly listening to or actually being open to the other. The ideal of rambling Socratic discussion in a search for truth is seldom experienced in our world. Let's just do what we do, be open to questions, remain gentle in the presence of disagreement, and let recruitment and persuasion occur on their own.

[62]

DISAGREEMENT

Trying to gain honor and respect
with wealth and lovely words
will only create the illusion
that we have accomplished something.

Instead, we work together in quiet commitment,
seeking nothing, speaking little,
seeing deeply into the soul,
and finding there no fault.

Disagreement is natural. It does not imply any fault or blame. As we do our work, let us see each other with clarity and charity, never worrying about how we are perceived, or about whether or not we are respected, or about who is right and who is wrong.

[63]

WITHOUT ADO

Let our action be without ado.
Clinging to nothing,
honoring the smallest efforts,
paying complete attention
to the present moment:
this is how we accomplish
the most momentous of tasks.

There is no frivolous or easy way
to ease the burden of the world.
It requires our dedication and willingness
all the way to the end.
Yet it must be accomplished
without excess strain and effort.

The essential paradox of "quiet activism" will face us every moment. Wanting to accomplish great things, we will return to the humble action that meets us in the moment. In this way, our muscles remain supple, our minds remain resilient, and our efforts remain effortless.

A SMALL STEP

The only step necessary
on the road to transformation
is the one right here, right now.
It is a small step,
easily taken.
It requires only the willingness
to lift the leg and extend the foot
a few short inches ahead,
then transfer the weight.
Easy.
Now, do it again.

Lay aside that small fearful thought. Don't listen to that voice that has been whispering lies into your ear your whole life. Don't plan great feats; just take the step that seems to be authentic, just, fair, and compassionate right now. What are you going to do *right now*? Read more in this book? Pick up another book? Check your messages? Every small thought and tiny action sets you on the road to...where?

IS THAT TRUE?

So many things we "know" are true
are simply conditioned beliefs,
used to keep us docile, compliant, and afraid.

The first step in transformation
is to learn that we do not know
what we think we know.
Then our not-knowing will create a space
in which true knowing might emerge.

The first step toward freedom
is ceasing to believe authority,
inside or out.
Then our nonbelief will open doors
to the actual experience of life.

From the time we take our first breath, cultural conditioning
begins its work of shaping us into the people we are "supposed to be." This conditioning is unavoidable, but it must
eventually be transcended by a growing, direct, "unfiltered"
awareness of life "as it is." This awareness is gained by en-
tering the most sacred and accepted areas of society with the
questions, "Oh, really?" and "Is that true?"

[66]

LEAD WITH HUMILITY

Leaders in this movement
must stay out of the way.
The more leaders try to lead,
the bigger obstacles they become.
When people are ready for transformation,
all a leader needs to do is carry water.
The greatest leaders throughout history
have led with quiet humility.
Their names are unknown.

Their honor is great.

We don't have to abandon our own understandings and goals or run about at the beck and call of everybody's whim. Our own wisdom and understanding guide us, but the change we work for is achieved by our willing service to those whose lives are on the line.

OUR WEAPONS

The Tao seems obscure and unknown.

It can't be marketed and sold.
No one can turn it into trivial polemics
designed to sway masses of people.

To do this work we must be bold.
It is compassion that keeps our boldness
from turning into ruthlessness.
We seek a society of sharing.
It is simplicity that keeps our sharing
from turning into control.
The road is long, dangerous, and tiring.
It is patience that keeps our fatigue
from turning into despair.

I understand those revolutionaries whose experiences led
them to armed conflict with those they identified as the
sources of oppression. I sometimes feel like taking up arms

myself. However, I am convinced that the battle will be won, not with force of arms, but with the power of compassion, simplicity, and patience. Still, the willingness to die in the service of transformation is as necessary for me as it has been for freedom fighters throughout history.

[68]

ANGER

Anger at injustice and tyranny is natural,
but it must not be the guiding force of action.
The aggressive energy of anger must transform itself
into calm and focused conduct.
In this way we confront
without confrontation,
triumph without defeating anyone,
and rebuild our world
without destroying it.

Most of us become involved in action because a specific situation tips our emotions into a burning outrage that such
a thing could be. For a period of time this anger lashes out
in all directions — blaming, confronting, and stirring up
righteous indignation. We enter into battle with gusto, but
we soon become bogged down in the complexity of social
forces we don't fully understand. Now we must let our anger become fluid energy, transforming the way we see and
think. This allows us to flow into the situation of the moment, to cleanse, nurture, and transform.

NO ENEMY

There is no room for "us" and "them"
in a world of peace and justice.
There will be people who, in their fear,
perceive us as the enemy,
who consider us deluded, dangerous,
and even evil.
Such thinking restricts creative action.

If two forces meet,
the one who has no enemy
will surely triumph.

A movement that has no enemy? Must there be some "evil-doer" we oppose? Can we oppose systems, habits, and structures without personifying them? Why create a personal enemy? The true "enemy" is the conditioned mind-set that oppresses all of us.

UNDERSTANDING ORIGINS

Change arises from the universe itself,
not from our intellectual pretenses.
If we understand these origins,
we understand ourselves,
and our actions flow with ease,
with energy, and with power.
If we are not aware of these origins,
we struggle much
and accomplish little.

It is fun to sit and discuss the abstract ideals of revolution. We argue with one another and study the theoretical structures of society. The intellectual energy this generates acts as an opiate for our discomfort. Everything happens within our stirred-up minds and dissipates before it turns to action. We are left with an exhausted feeling, as if we have really accomplished something, but nothing changes.

HEALING

If we presume to know
the roots of society's suffering,
but do not know our own,
we don't know anything at all.
If we refuse to see suffering's inner origins,
we will never heal the outer symptoms.
If we awaken to these inner origins,
we will become a healing force.

Transformation is an inward process that manifests in outward actions. Actions that don't arise from this inner transformation will fail because they are based on the very premises that caused the disease in the first place. Of course, we try to treat the symptoms of injustice while we search for cures for the disease itself. Symptom treatment is part of healing. But keep searching for the root causes...and don't be afraid to look within your own mind.

TRUST OURSELVES

When people fail to trust themselves,
they turn to authority,
and authority gladly reinforces
their lack of self-regard.
When people cherish themselves,
authority cannot gain advantage.
The natural course of things
brings dignity to all.
No one grows weary.
No one is excluded.

When we learn to value ourselves, our structures will truly serve. Self-doubt and self-hate make us fall prey to the structures built by others. "Trust us," they say, then they drain our resources into their pockets, leaving us poor and even more bereft of confidence. The circle never ends until we choose to end it.

A HIDDEN PATH

The path ahead is hidden.
Unknown obstacles and troubles
we can't foresee await us.
We'll do the best we can,
but both harm and benefit will come,
and we must accept them both.
Each is essential to our journey.

We will be patient, quiet, and present
to everything that arises.
The mysteries along our way are numerous,
yet we will never lose our way.
Who can predict the path of the Tao?

I doubt this revolution will culminate in a victory parade
with waving flags and marching soldiers. It will be a series
of small triumphs, hardly noticed at the time. Often there
will be defeats as well. Each triumph, each defeat, will work
together to weave the net of freedom that will cover the land
at last.

THE PRICE

When death and loss are feared
and contaminate the mind,
freedom is nowhere to be found.
Every action becomes controlled
by subtle messages of fear.
We bow and pay the price
to those who promise safety,
comfort, and prosperity.
But this fear of death and loss
leads only to more death and loss.

When death and loss become a natural part of life,
neither feared nor sought,
true freedom comes into being.

Our work must be nonviolent in order to succeed, but that
does not mean that it will be without sacrifice. It will entail
immense sacrifice, discipline, and even the willingness to
die. Make no mistake, we may be Taoist revolutionaries, but
we are revolutionaries nonetheless.

CONTROLLED BY WANTING

Society's need for control
is driving us to madness.
Watched, tagged, followed, polled,
exploited, badgered, harassed, and pushed
into niches, slots, and cubicles
for the benefit of unknown powers,
we are inches from exploding.

Wanting more and more,
and fearing more and more,
form the chains that hold us prisoner.
No longer striving to be the people
we are told we're supposed to be,
we will find, at last, that we are free.

We have come to believe that stress, strain, fear, and the struggle to get ahead are normal — simply part of the modern world. That belief allows those who dangle the trinkets of our culture before our eyes, whispering that we truly need and want these baubles, to control every aspect of our daily lives — what we do, watch, buy, and think.

LIKE BAMBOO

Before we are taught to fear,
to desire, and to strive for success,
we are naturally tender, compassionate,
flexible, and alive.
By the time we take our place
as cogs in the gears of commerce,
we are stiff, armored, rigid, and dying.

Flexibility is the sign of life.
Stiffness is the sign of death.
Our ability to change our plans,
adjust our strategies, and bend in the wind
will be our saving strength.

We are like the bamboo shoot, strong yet supple. Unlike the rootless tumbleweed, the bamboo shoot can bend and spring back with ease because it is connected at the roots with all the other bamboo shoots in the grove. A bamboo grove is just one plant! We are part of one great river, and we can move, think, and live with a sense of flowing ease.

BALANCE

The Way of the Tao is balance:
Where there is too much,
it takes away and gives
to where there is too little.
The way of society is otherwise:
Where there is too much,
it adds even more by taking
from where there is too little.
This is madness.

This is the way we use our resources:
we add to where there is too little
and withhold from where there is too much.
In this, we are like the Tao
and will never be depleted.

The solution is not communism. Neither is it capitalism as
we know it. Most of our evolutionary history was played
out in small wandering tribes or small settled villages. We
naturally cared for one another and found our own unique
place within our family, tribe, and village. We depended on

cooperation and empathy in order to survive. Sharing, caring, and mutual support were not moral virtues but natural virtues — part of the essence of who we were. We had to be taught, educated, and conditioned by massive social forces over a period of hundreds of years in order to become as isolated, individualistic, separate, and fearful as we are.

FLUID POWER

Nothing can stop water as it journeys
from rainfall on the mountainside
in streams and rivers to the sea.
Dams of stone and concrete,
standing rigid in its path,
are no match for its fluid power.

When we meet the rigid powers,
so confident of their strength,
we flow around,
pour over,
seep under,
or evaporate and rain down
on the other side.
Nothing can stop the river of revolution
from reaching its ocean home.

There will be great temptation to mimic the strength of our
opposition: to pick up rocks and guns and meet rigidity with
rigidity. This will bring failure even in victory for the rigidity will remain, and we will become oppressors in our
turn. Only the fluid power of the River of Tao will both
overcome obstacles and nurture the land.

[79]

NO BLAME

We cannot build a society
on a foundation of blame.
If the "one percent" is blamed and shamed,
the pain of resentment will never end.
We will wind up building guillotines,
and soon our own necks
will be on the block.

The Tao will restore its natural balance
without the use of either blame or punishment.
Those who have been rewarded for their greed
and those who have been shamed for their need
will together be freed from blame
and together live in harmony.

It is so easy for me, when I get on my mental soapbox, to
find easy targets for my anger — the Media, the Govern-
ment, the Rich, the Enemy hidden out there somewhere.
Yet my concepts of groups and organizations are insubstan-
tial wisps of thought within my mind. The reality is simply
individual people who are caught in the web of their own
conditioned minds and acting out whatever story they have
learned.

AFTER THE REVOLUTION

Progress will not remain
our most important product.
Going faster and having more
will be of little interest.
Enjoyment of the moment
will temper the power
of the marketplace.
Simple pleasures will return
and fill our world with natural joy.

We will no longer waste our time
in pursuit of illusions and fantasies.
There will be time for love
and time for peace;
time to pay attention to children
and time to sip our tea and wine
in quiet contentment.
Death will no longer be a problem
because we will have fully lived.

The desire for "more" is carefully cultivated and exploited.
It began in our evolutionary history with the simple need
to provide the security of food and shelter. Now artificial

desire and dissatisfaction drive the engines of our culture. Contentment is dismissed as lazy or apathetic. We are not seeking a place for all on the hamster wheel of commerce. We are seeking the elimination of the wheel entirely.

TRUTH?

Every concept that arises in our brains
falls short of the truth.
When we form words about these concepts,
the truth recedes still further.
We cannot rely on words or books
to convince or change the world.
We can only demonstrate
by the simplicity of our lives,
the generosity of our spirits,
the acceptance in our hearts,
and the service of our lives
that a Taoist Transformation
is the Truth.

My words stumble. I have tried to make them as true as possible, yet, of necessity, they fall far short. We all know the
Truth within the heart of the Cosmos, of the Tao. I hope
I have pointed in that direction. I hope my words have
communicated some sense of the paradox of urgency and

serenity that coexist within me. May everyone who, at this moment, is reading these words that I am writing in this, my own present moment, understand that we are not separated by anything real — time and space included. Peace and joy to us always.

[AFTERWORD]

With this little book, I have added another fourteen thousand or so words to the flood of words in our culture, all the while knowing that words are dangerous and misleading. I believe Lao-Tzu's sentiment expressed in chapter 56 of the Tao Te Ching, "Those who speak do not know. Those who know do not speak." Writing is, of course, a form of speaking. Why then do I continue to speak that which cannot be spoken and write that which cannot be written?

I write because it is my craft and art. I have nothing else to offer in way of return for the privilege of life, and it has indeed been a privilege. I try to express my gratitude by being awake to the direct experience of this life. I owe to life the effort to see it as it is rather than through the conditioned filters of my mind. Then I try to write what I see.

I'd never considered myself a revolutionary. I lived through the sixties without really understanding the counterculture movement of the time. I graduated from university as an electronic engineer and followed my conditioned mind down a conventional path of family and career. As a research scientist with the navy, I avoided the firsthand horrors of Vietnam and thus did not have the wake-up call that many of my generation experienced.

Without filling in the biographical details of my long journey, suffice it to say that I have gradually, somewhat unconsciously, become a dedicated revolutionary — a quiet activist, not really a political activist. Following the advice of Lao-Tzu, whose teachings are perhaps the most revolutionary teachings in history, I try to stay hidden and let the movement of the Tao accomplish transformation in its own fashion.

I am, however, as are we all, an integral part of this Tao movement toward balance, and I am compelled to play my own small role. I am a writer, perhaps a poet. Writers who write for revolutionary purposes, however, cease being writers and become propagandists. My role is not to convince or persuade but to use my craft to express the heart of the Tao as clearly and aesthetically as possible. I believe a transformative revolution is inevitable, but it will occur in its own manner, in its own time. I am a seed planter, a tender of a garden of words. What grows from the seeds must grow from its own inner nature, the nature of the Tao. I can neither stop the wheel of Yin and Yang from turning nor force it to turn faster or slower according to my wishes.

The Tao will always restore equilibrium to the Cosmos. The mindless consumption, distraction, greed, fear, and ecological disaster we have wrought as a species will be brought into balance one way or another. We will return to simplicity, right livelihood, and a caring relationship with the Earth — either by mindful choice or by apocalyptic force. It seems to be up to us. I offer this question to you and to all of us: What might life look like after the Tao transforms it? Let's imagine it as best we can. Then, using these images, let's begin now to live that way.

Let's forget about what "they should be doing" and turn our attention to entirely new approaches. Each time we become aware of the pain, injustice, and insanity in the systems around us, let's brainstorm creative ideas for doing things in a different manner. We don't have to justify, defend, or enact these ideas; simply brainstorm them and bring them into the open. Let's discuss them with one another, and perhaps one out of one hundred will strike a chord in someone somewhere and another small step toward healing and justice will emerge.

We will all die no matter what we choose to do. We can choose to die in comfortable compliance with culture, clutching our trinkets and toys, looking back on a life of fear and desperation. Or we can choose to die in the joyful service of a vision, clinging to nothing, looking back on a life of courage and integrity, a life well spent. We have the marvelous opportunity to support one another in living our lives in surprising, authentic, and joyful ways.

Blessings,
Bill Martin

[ACKNOWLEDGMENTS]

Thank you, Nancy, my love.
Thank you, Barbara Moulton, my friend and agent.
Thank you to all who have walked with me along the Tao.
Blessings to my children and grandchildren,
who will have to live this revolution more fully than I.
And, well…just thank you, period.

[ABOUT THE AUTHOR]

William Martin is an award-winning author whose work expresses the practical wisdom and inspiration of Taoist thought for contemporary readers. He is the spouse of Nancy, the father of Lara and John, and the grandfather of Jillian and Andrew.

A native of California, Bill graduated from the University of California at Berkeley with a degree in electronic engineering. After four years working for the navy as a research scientist, he returned to graduate school. He earned a master's degree from Western Theological Seminary in Holland, Michigan. He did not find himself fitting within the Christian church clergy structure, so guided by his love of the Tao Te Ching, he began to seek his own way. He spent two decades in private practice as a marriage and family counselor in Phoenix, Arizona, and taught counseling for many years at Rio Salado College in Phoenix and Tempe. He has been a student of the Tao for four decades.

In 1998 Bill and Nancy decided to simplify their lives, so they sold most of their possessions, left their careers, gathered their remaining belongings into a five-by-eight-foot U-Haul trailer, and moved to the Oregon Coast. Nancy worked at a small inn, and Bill wrote a book. In 1999, after a year of strolling along the beaches, walking through the forests, and feeling the intense joy of the natural world, they moved to Northern California. They live a somewhat private existence, connecting with their close friends and with their individual work. They walk, read, enjoy qigong, and cherish their life together. Nancy is a traditional bookbinder, restoring old books and creating hand-bound editions of new ones (www.nwbookbinding.com). Bill continues to write (www.taoistliving.com) and paint in the Taoist tradition.